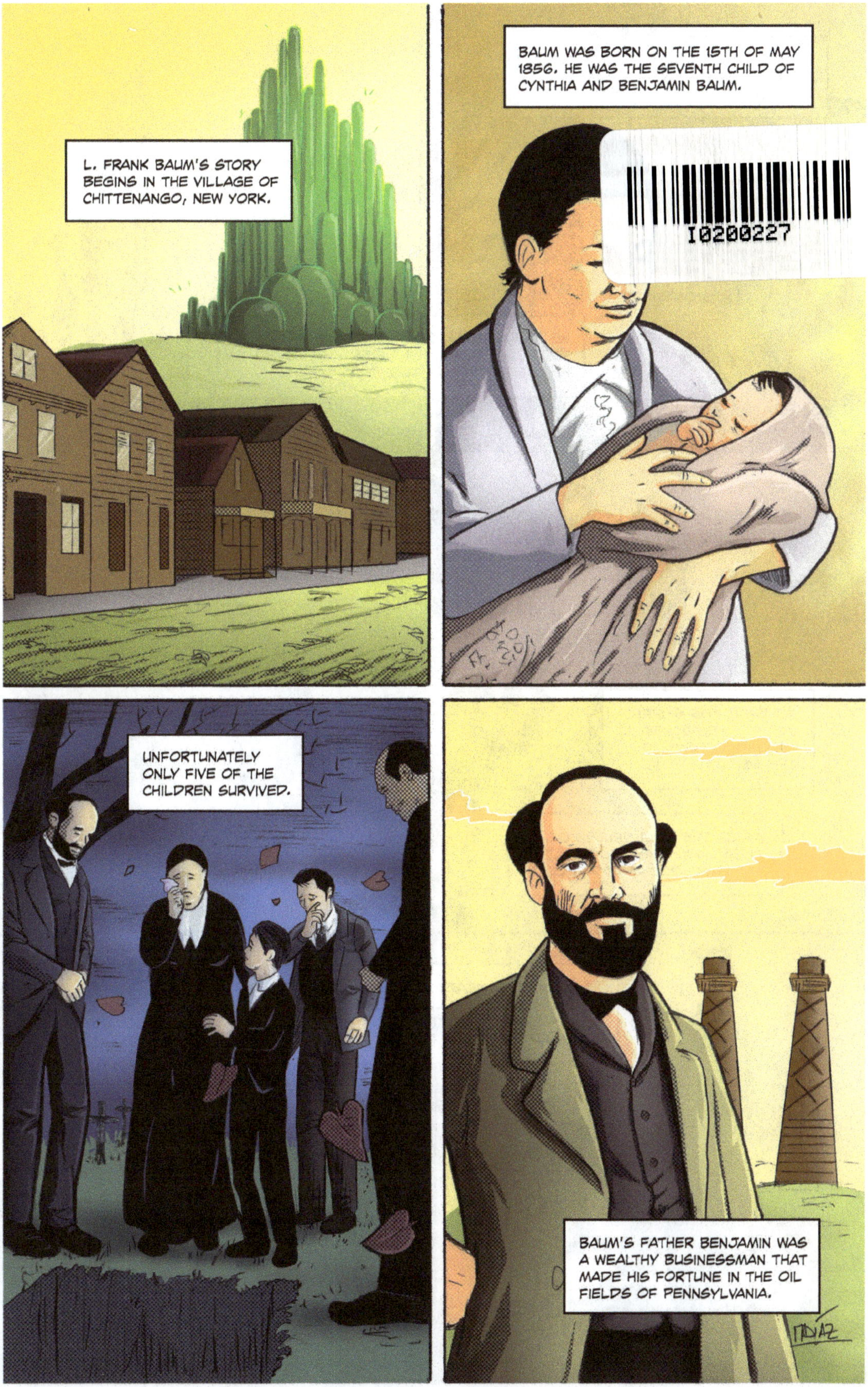
L. FRANK BAUM'S STORY BEGINS IN THE VILLAGE OF CHITTENANGO, NEW YORK.
BAUM WAS BORN ON THE 15TH OF MAY 1856. HE WAS THE SEVENTH CHILD OF CYNTHIA AND BENJAMIN BAUM.
UNFORTUNATELY ONLY FIVE OF THE CHILDREN SURVIVED.
BAUM'S FATHER BENJAMIN WAS A WEALTHY BUSINESSMAN THAT MADE HIS FORTUNE IN THE OIL FIELDS OF PENNSYLVANIA.

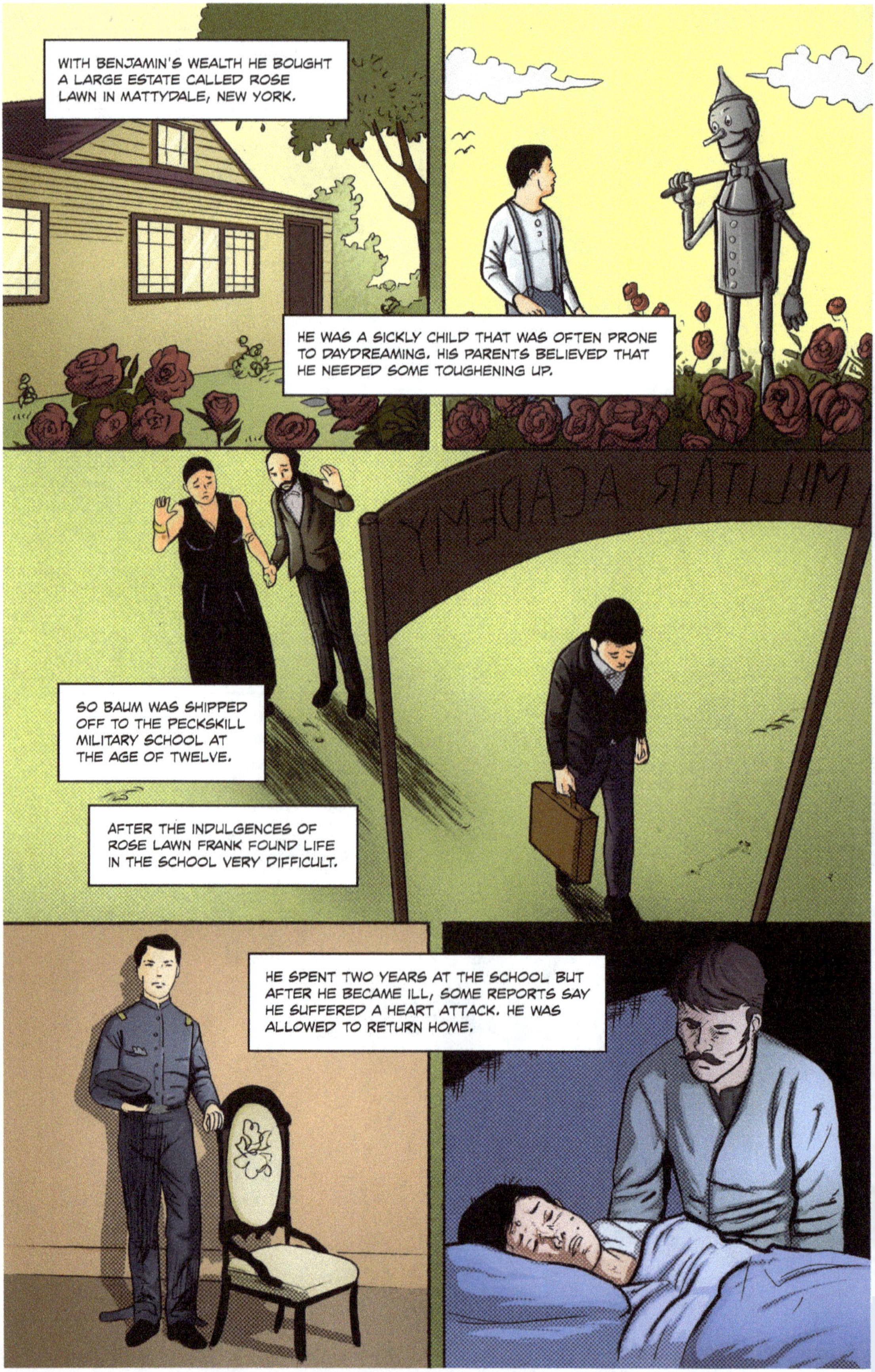
WITH BENJAMIN'S WEALTH HE BOUGHT A LARGE ESTATE CALLED ROSE LAWN IN MATTYDALE, NEW YORK.
HE WAS A SICKLY CHILD THAT WAS OFTEN PRONE TO DAYDREAMING. HIS PARENTS BELIEVED THAT HE NEEDED SOME TOUGHENING UP.
SO BAUM WAS SHIPPED OFF TO THE PECKSKILL MILITARY SCHOOL AT THE AGE OF TWELVE.
AFTER THE INDULGENCES OF ROSE LAWN FRANK FOUND LIFE IN THE SCHOOL VERY DIFFICULT.
HE SPENT TWO YEARS AT THE SCHOOL BUT AFTER HE BECAME ILL, SOME REPORTS SAY HE SUFFERED A HEART ATTACK. HE WAS ALLOWED TO RETURN HOME.

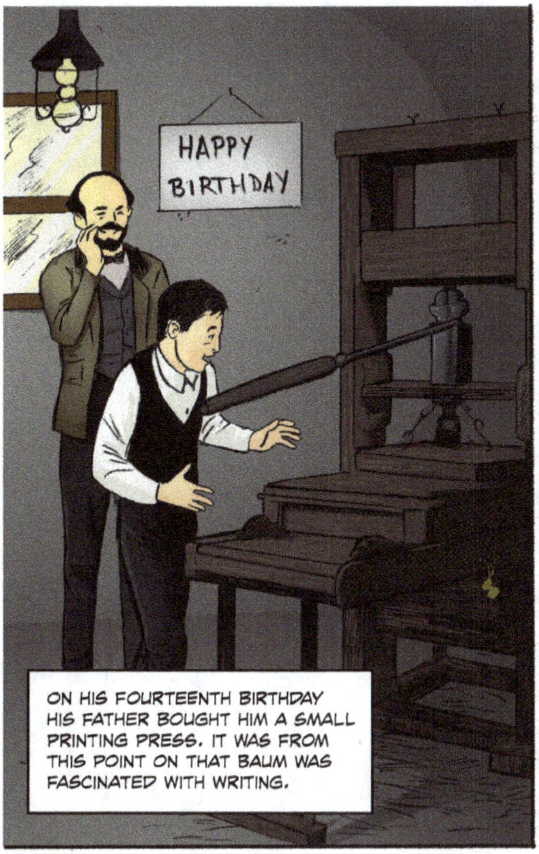
HAPPY BIRTHDAY
ON HIS FOURTEENTH BIRTHDAY HIS FATHER BOUGHT HIM A SMALL PRINTING PRESS. IT WAS FROM THIS POINT ON THAT BAUM WAS FASCINATED WITH WRITING.

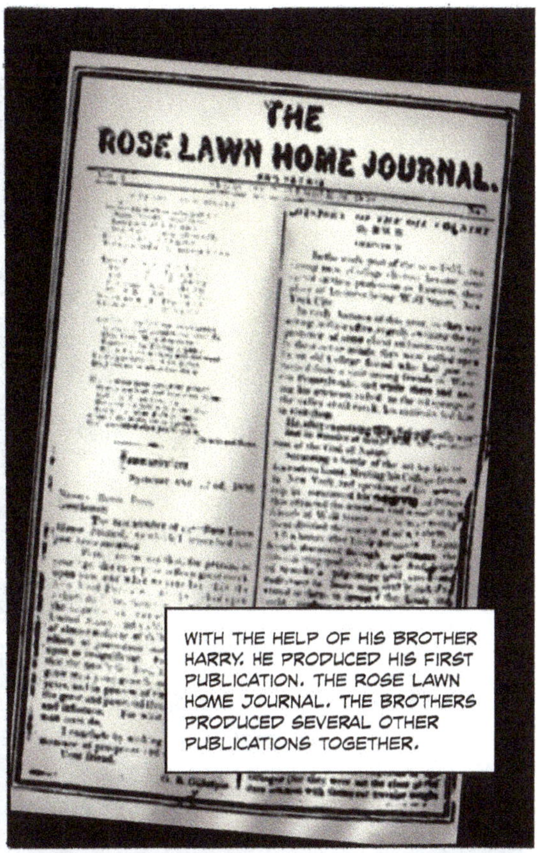
THE ROSE LAWN HOME JOURNAL.
WITH THE HELP OF HIS BROTHER HARRY, HE PRODUCED HIS FIRST PUBLICATION, THE ROSE LAWN HOME JOURNAL. THE BROTHERS PRODUCED SEVERAL OTHER PUBLICATIONS TOGETHER.

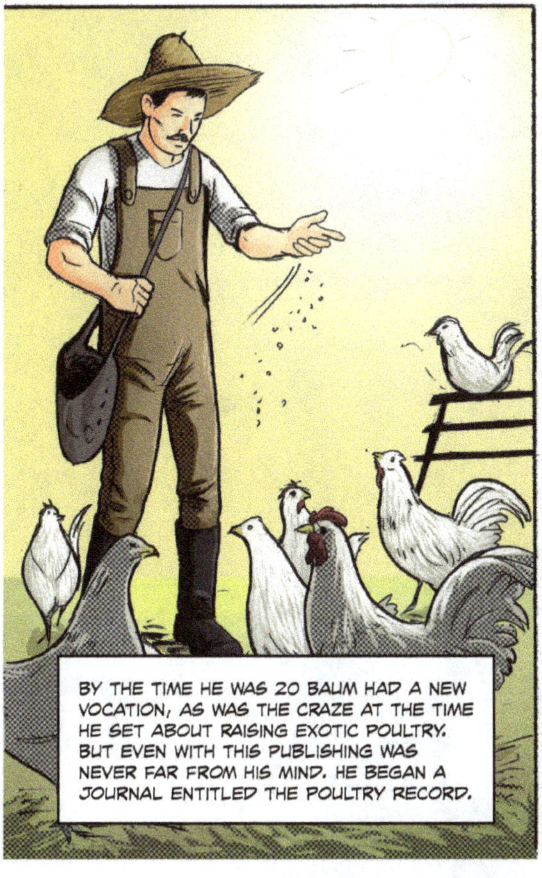
BY THE TIME HE WAS 20 BAUM HAD A NEW VOCATION, AS WAS THE CRAZE AT THE TIME HE SET ABOUT RAISING EXOTIC POULTRY. BUT EVEN WITH THIS PUBLISHING WAS NEVER FAR FROM HIS MIND. HE BEGAN A JOURNAL ENTITLED THE POULTRY RECORD.

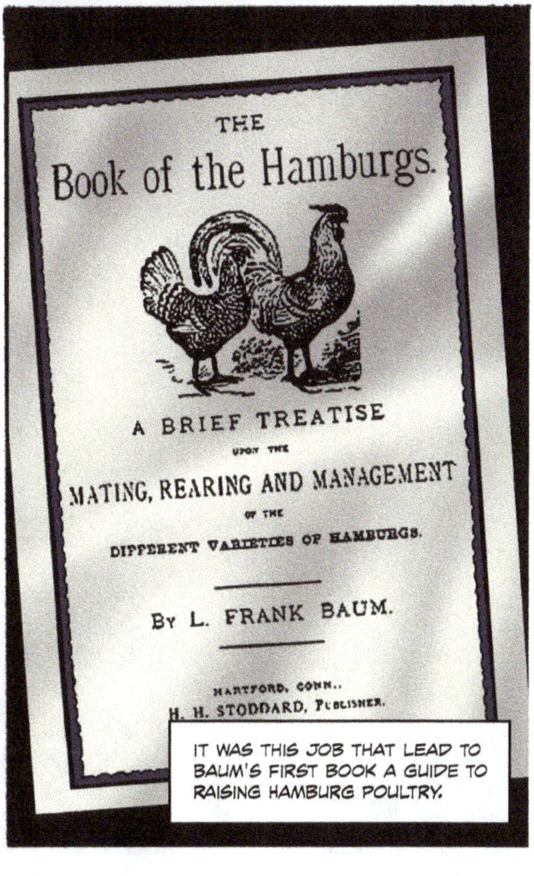
THE
Book of the Hamburgs.
A BRIEF TREATISE
UPON THE
MATING, REARING AND MANAGEMENT
OF THE
DIFFERENT VARIETIES OF HAMBURGS.
BY L. FRANK BAUM.
HARTFORD, CONN.,
H. H. STODDARD, PUBLISHER.
IT WAS THIS JOB THAT LEAD TO BAUM'S FIRST BOOK A GUIDE TO RAISING HAMBURG POULTRY.

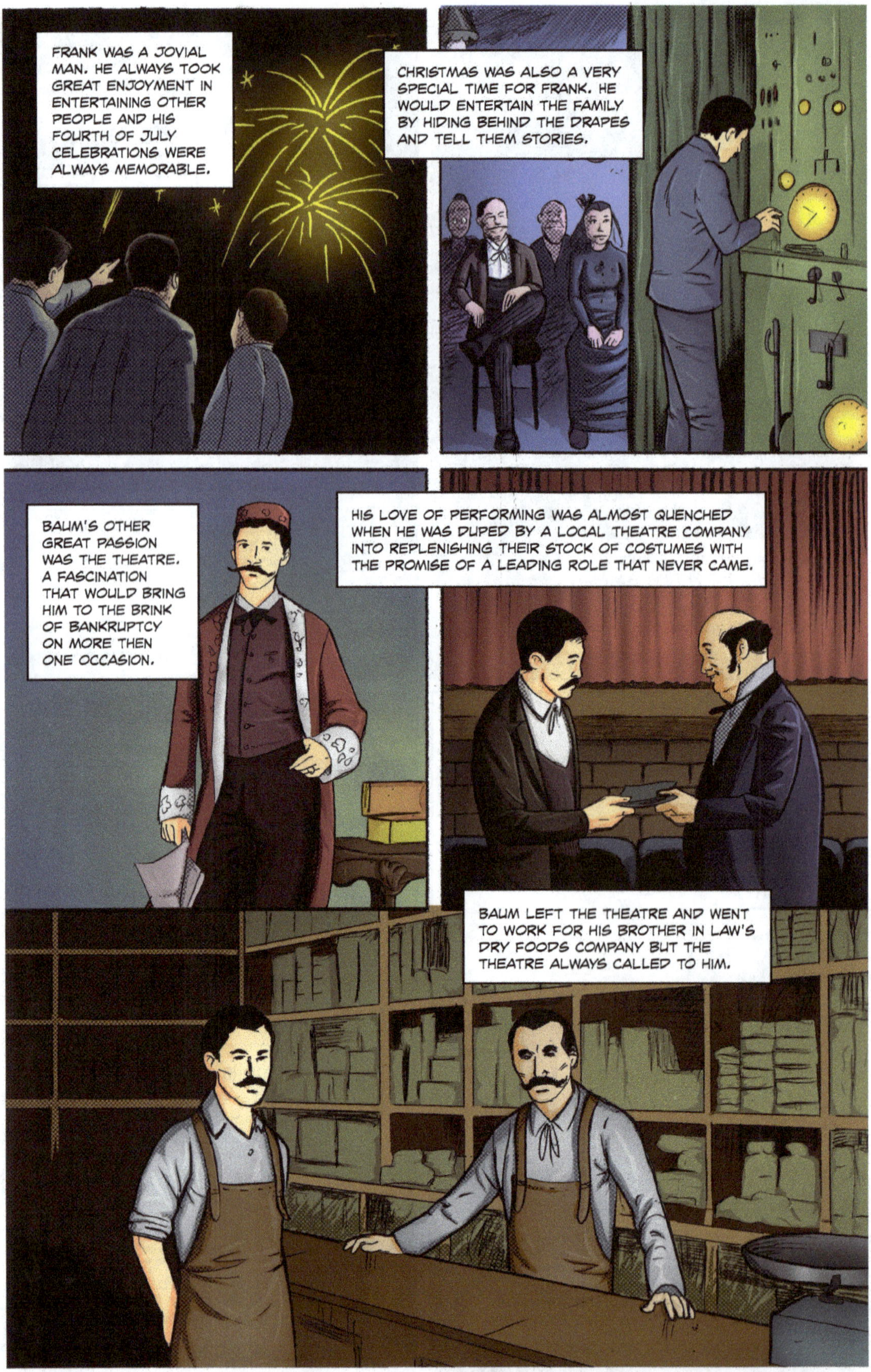
FRANK WAS A JOVIAL MAN. HE ALWAYS TOOK GREAT ENJOYMENT IN ENTERTAINING OTHER PEOPLE AND HIS FOURTH OF JULY CELEBRATIONS WERE ALWAYS MEMORABLE.
CHRISTMAS WAS ALSO A VERY SPECIAL TIME FOR FRANK. HE WOULD ENTERTAIN THE FAMILY BY HIDING BEHIND THE DRAPES AND TELL THEM STORIES.
BAUM'S OTHER GREAT PASSION WAS THE THEATRE. A FASCINATION THAT WOULD BRING HIM TO THE BRINK OF BANKRUPTCY ON MORE THEN ONE OCCASION.
HIS LOVE OF PERFORMING WAS ALMOST QUENCHED WHEN HE WAS DUPED BY A LOCAL THEATRE COMPANY INTO REPLENISHING THEIR STOCK OF COSTUMES WITH THE PROMISE OF A LEADING ROLE THAT NEVER CAME.
BAUM LEFT THE THEATRE AND WENT TO WORK FOR HIS BROTHER IN LAW'S DRY FOODS COMPANY BUT THE THEATRE ALWAYS CALLED TO HIM.

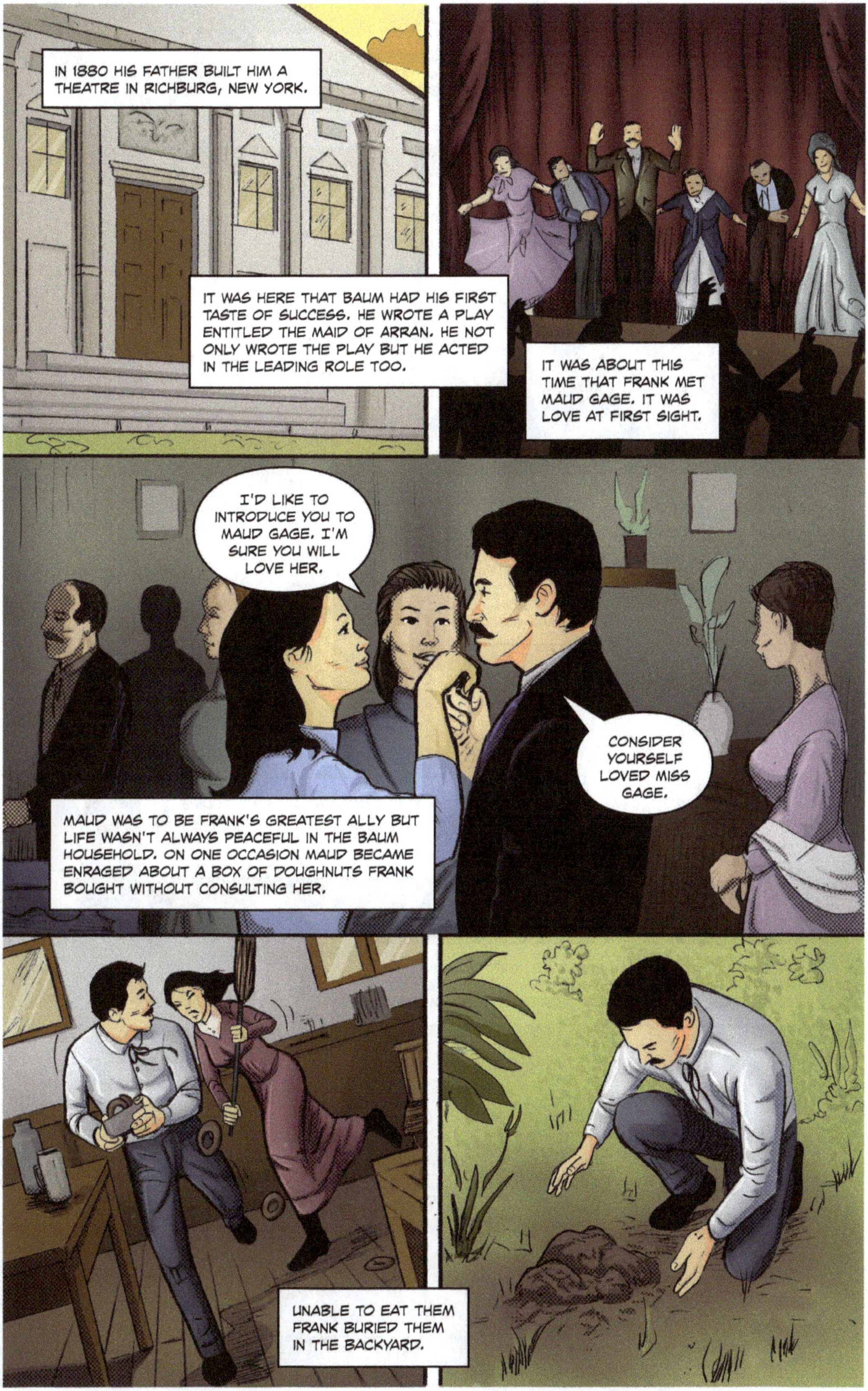
IN 1880 HIS FATHER BUILT HIM A THEATRE IN RICHBURG, NEW YORK.
IT WAS HERE THAT BAUM HAD HIS FIRST TASTE OF SUCCESS. HE WROTE A PLAY ENTITLED THE MAID OF ARRAN. HE NOT ONLY WROTE THE PLAY BUT HE ACTED IN THE LEADING ROLE TOO.
IT WAS ABOUT THIS TIME THAT FRANK MET MAUD GAGE. IT WAS LOVE AT FIRST SIGHT.
I'D LIKE TO INTRODUCE YOU TO MAUD GAGE. I'M SURE YOU WILL LOVE HER.
CONSIDER YOURSELF LOVED MISS GAGE.
MAUD WAS TO BE FRANK'S GREATEST ALLY BUT LIFE WASN'T ALWAYS PEACEFUL IN THE BAUM HOUSEHOLD. ON ONE OCCASION MAUD BECAME ENRAGED ABOUT A BOX OF DOUGHNUTS FRANK BOUGHT WITHOUT CONSULTING HER.
UNABLE TO EAT THEM FRANK BURIED THEM IN THE BACKYARD.

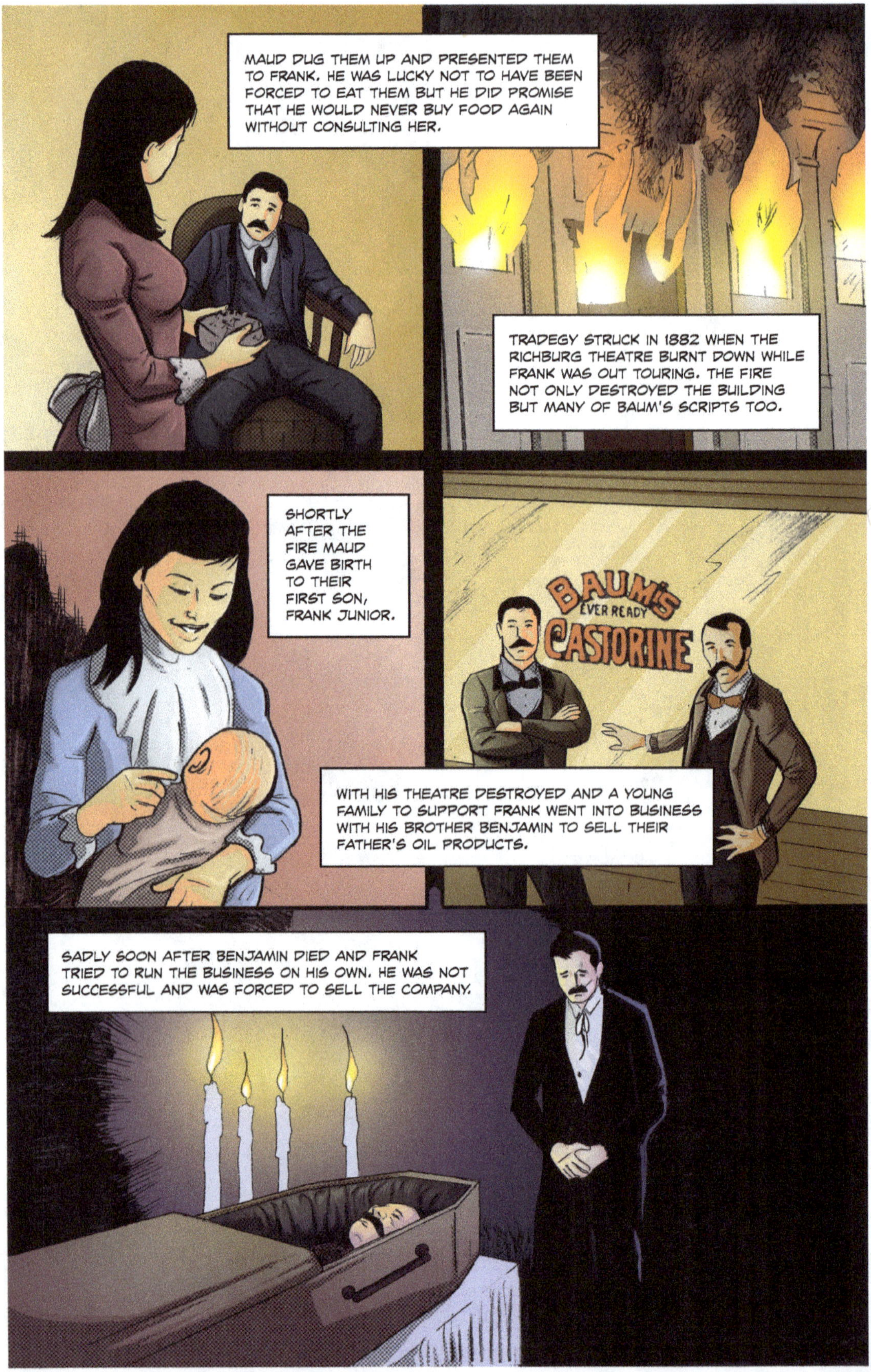
MAUD DUG THEM UP AND PRESENTED THEM TO FRANK. HE WAS LUCKY NOT TO HAVE BEEN FORCED TO EAT THEM BUT HE DID PROMISE THAT HE WOULD NEVER BUY FOOD AGAIN WITHOUT CONSULTING HER.
TRADEGY STRUCK IN 1882 WHEN THE RICHBURG THEATRE BURNT DOWN WHILE FRANK WAS OUT TOURING. THE FIRE NOT ONLY DESTROYED THE BUILDING BUT MANY OF BAUM'S SCRIPTS TOO.
SHORTLY AFTER THE FIRE MAUD GAVE BIRTH TO THEIR FIRST SON, FRANK JUNIOR.
BAUM'S EVER READY CASTORINE
WITH HIS THEATRE DESTROYED AND A YOUNG FAMILY TO SUPPORT FRANK WENT INTO BUSINESS WITH HIS BROTHER BENJAMIN TO SELL THEIR FATHER'S OIL PRODUCTS.
SADLY SOON AFTER BENJAMIN DIED AND FRANK TRIED TO RUN THE BUSINESS ON HIS OWN. HE WAS NOT SUCCESSFUL AND WAS FORCED TO SELL THE COMPANY.

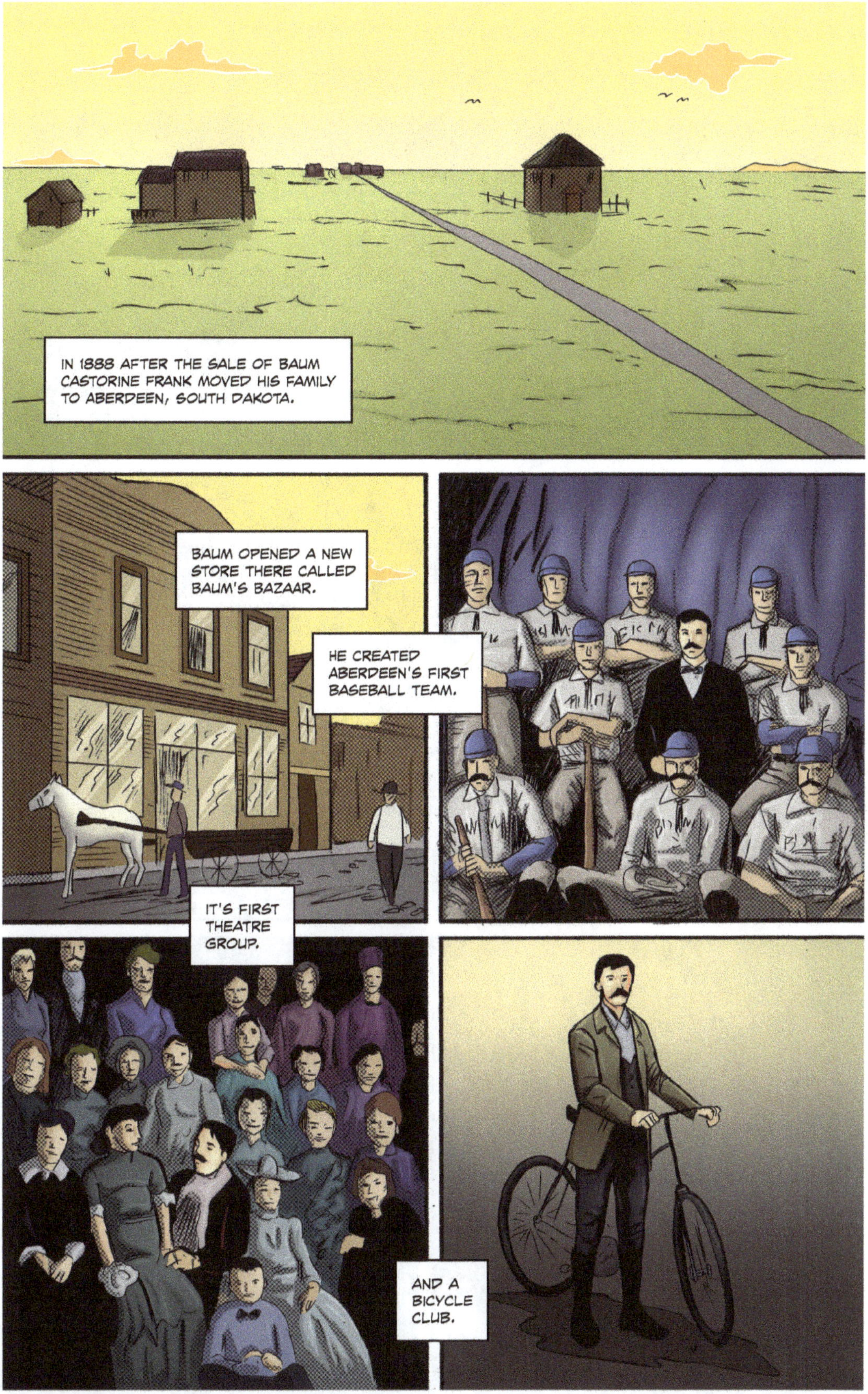
IN 1888 AFTER THE SALE OF BAUM CASTORINE FRANK MOVED HIS FAMILY TO ABERDEEN, SOUTH DAKOTA.
BAUM OPENED A NEW STORE THERE CALLED BAUM'S BAZAAR.
HE CREATED ABERDEEN'S FIRST BASEBALL TEAM.
IT'S FIRST THEATRE GROUP.
AND A BICYCLE CLUB.

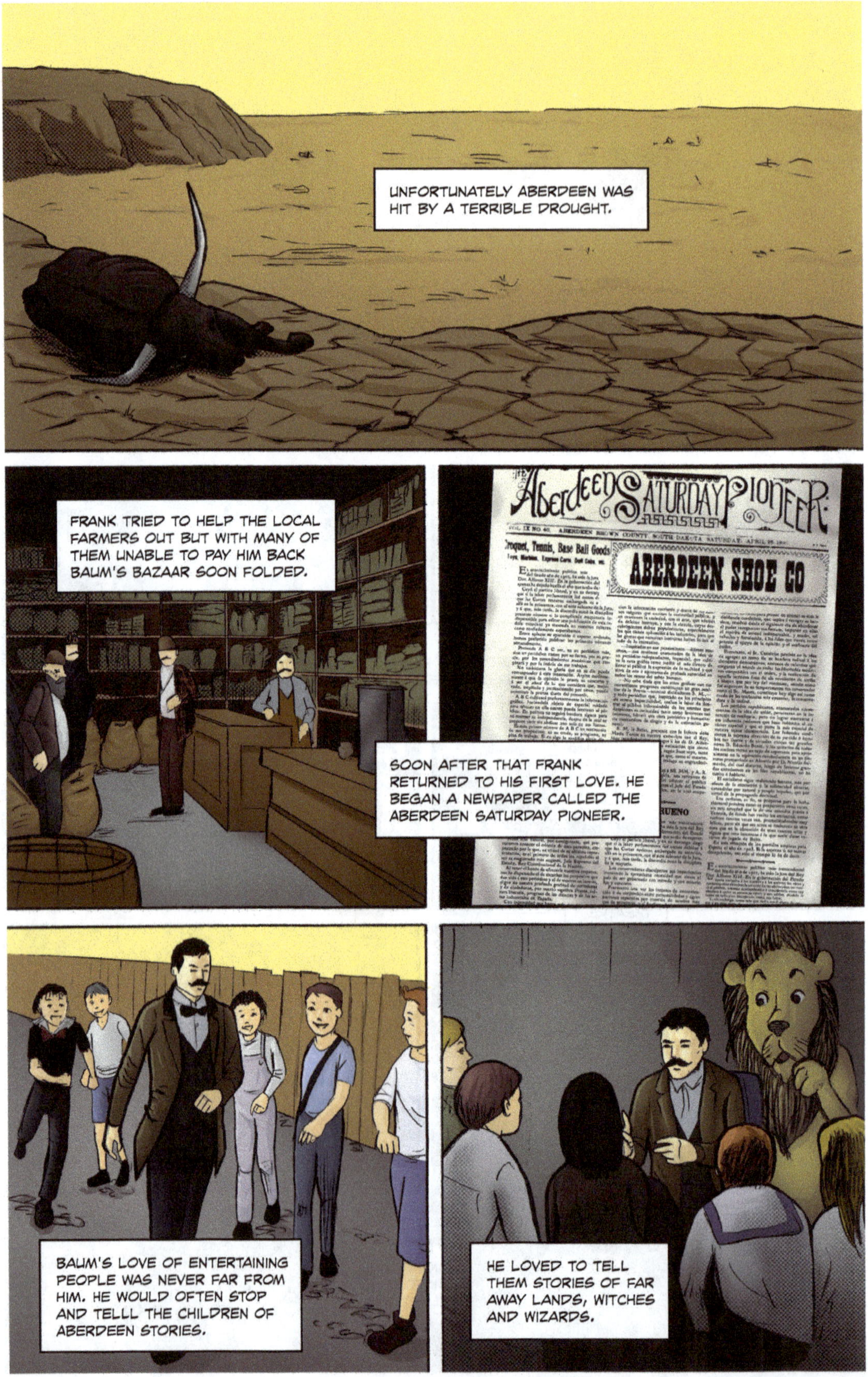
UNFORTUNATELY ABERDEEN WAS HIT BY A TERRIBLE DROUGHT.
FRANK TRIED TO HELP THE LOCAL FARMERS OUT BUT WITH MANY OF THEM UNABLE TO PAY HIM BACK BAUM'S BAZAAR SOON FOLDED.
Aberdeen Saturday Pioneer
Croquet, Tennis, Base Ball Goods
ABERDEEN SHOE CO
SOON AFTER THAT FRANK RETURNED TO HIS FIRST LOVE. HE BEGAN A NEWPAPER CALLED THE ABERDEEN SATURDAY PIONEER.
BAUM'S LOVE OF ENTERTAINING PEOPLE WAS NEVER FAR FROM HIM. HE WOULD OFTEN STOP AND TELLL THE CHILDREN OF ABERDEEN STORIES.
HE LOVED TO TELL THEM STORIES OF FAR AWAY LANDS, WITCHES AND WIZARDS.

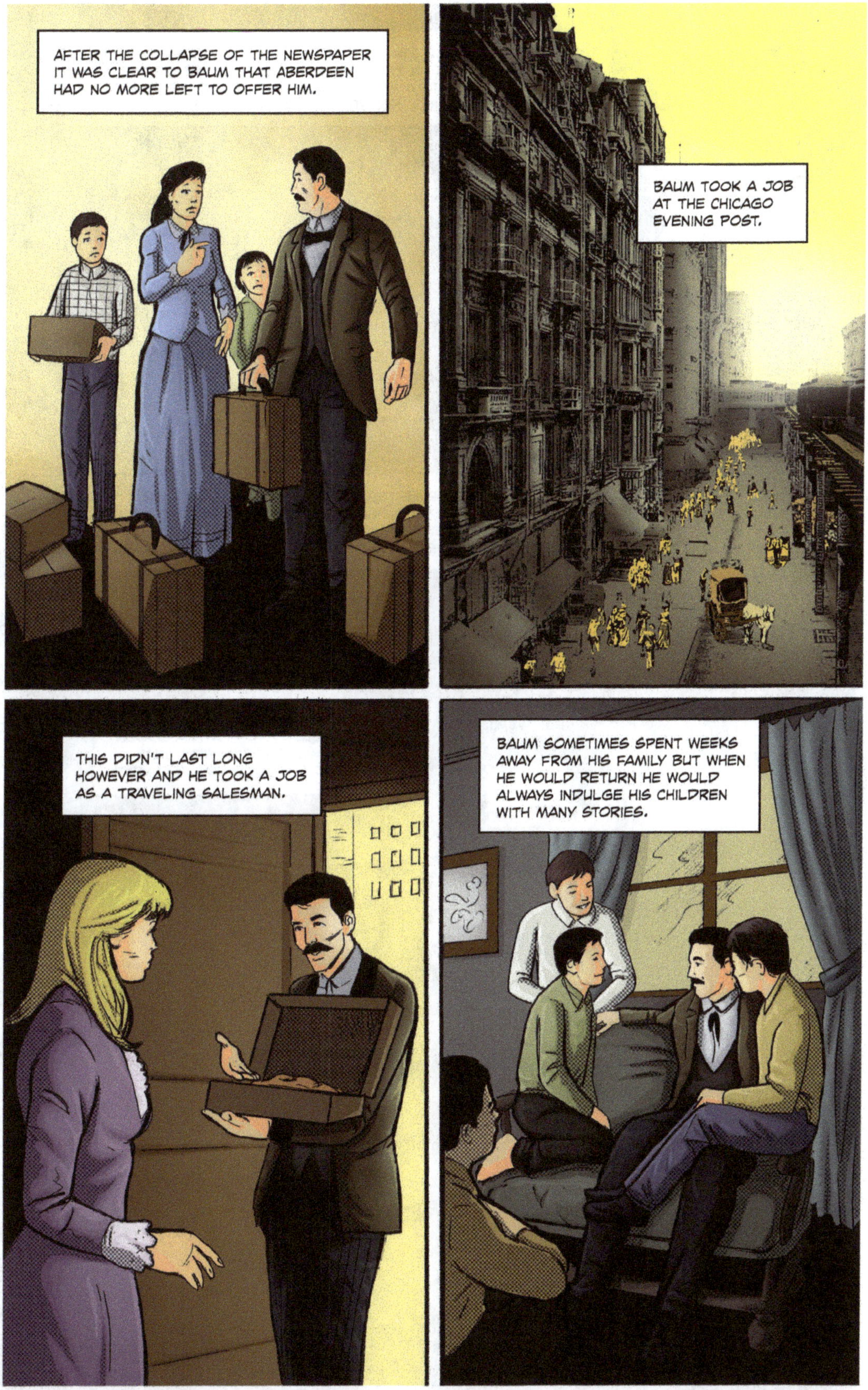
AFTER THE COLLAPSE OF THE NEWSPAPER IT WAS CLEAR TO BAUM THAT ABERDEEN HAD NO MORE LEFT TO OFFER HIM.
BAUM TOOK A JOB AT THE CHICAGO EVENING POST.
THIS DIDN'T LAST LONG HOWEVER AND HE TOOK A JOB AS A TRAVELING SALESMAN.
BAUM SOMETIMES SPENT WEEKS AWAY FROM HIS FAMILY BUT WHEN HE WOULD RETURN HE WOULD ALWAYS INDULGE HIS CHILDREN WITH MANY STORIES.

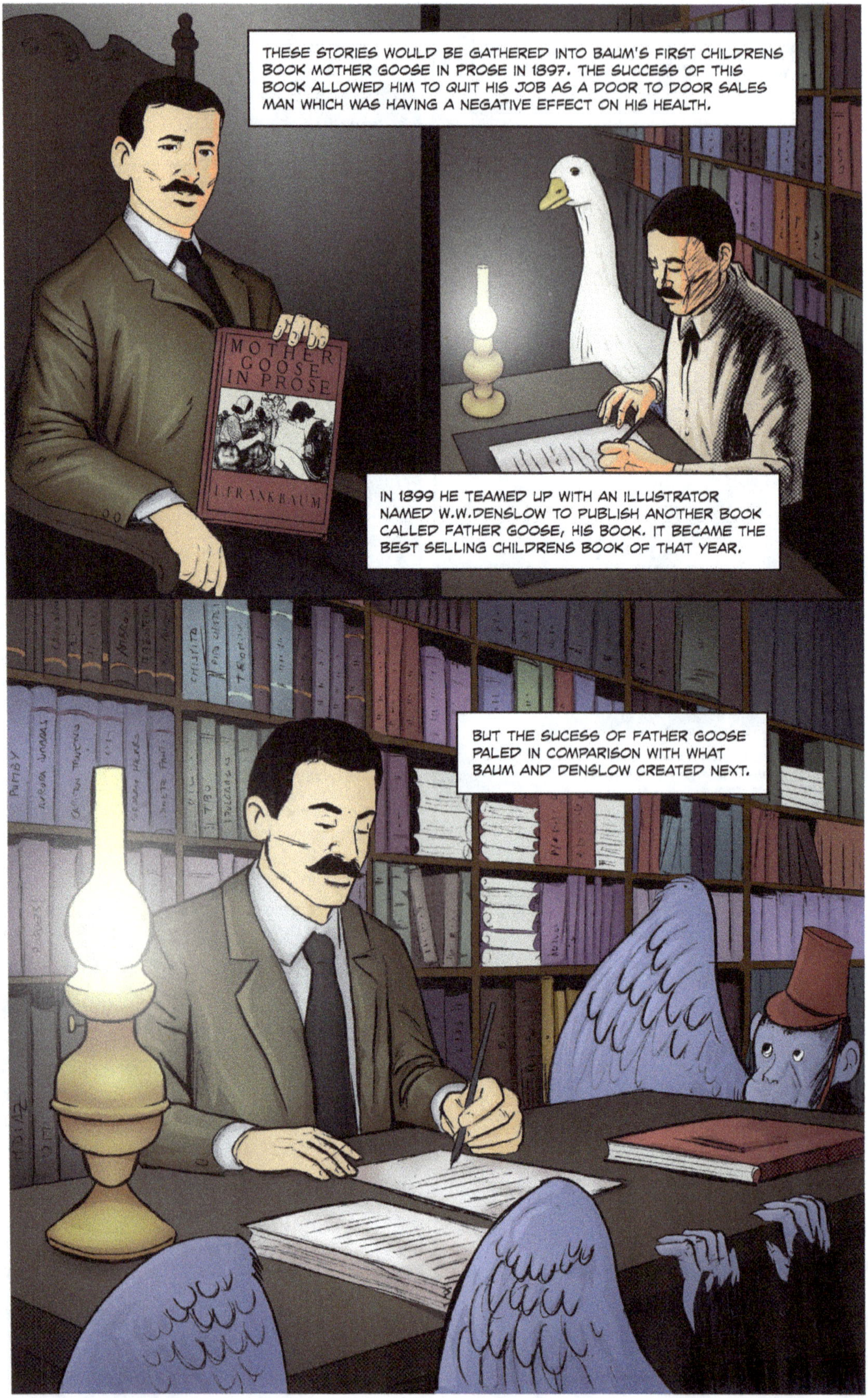
THESE STORIES WOULD BE GATHERED INTO BAUM'S FIRST CHILDRENS BOOK MOTHER GOOSE IN PROSE IN 1897. THE SUCCESS OF THIS BOOK ALLOWED HIM TO QUIT HIS JOB AS A DOOR TO DOOR SALES MAN WHICH WAS HAVING A NEGATIVE EFFECT ON HIS HEALTH.
MOTHER GOOSE IN PROSE
L.FRANK BAUM
IN 1899 HE TEAMED UP WITH AN ILLUSTRATOR NAMED W.W.DENSLOW TO PUBLISH ANOTHER BOOK CALLED FATHER GOOSE, HIS BOOK. IT BECAME THE BEST SELLING CHILDRENS BOOK OF THAT YEAR.
BUT THE SUCESS OF FATHER GOOSE PALED IN COMPARISON WITH WHAT BAUM AND DENSLOW CREATED NEXT.

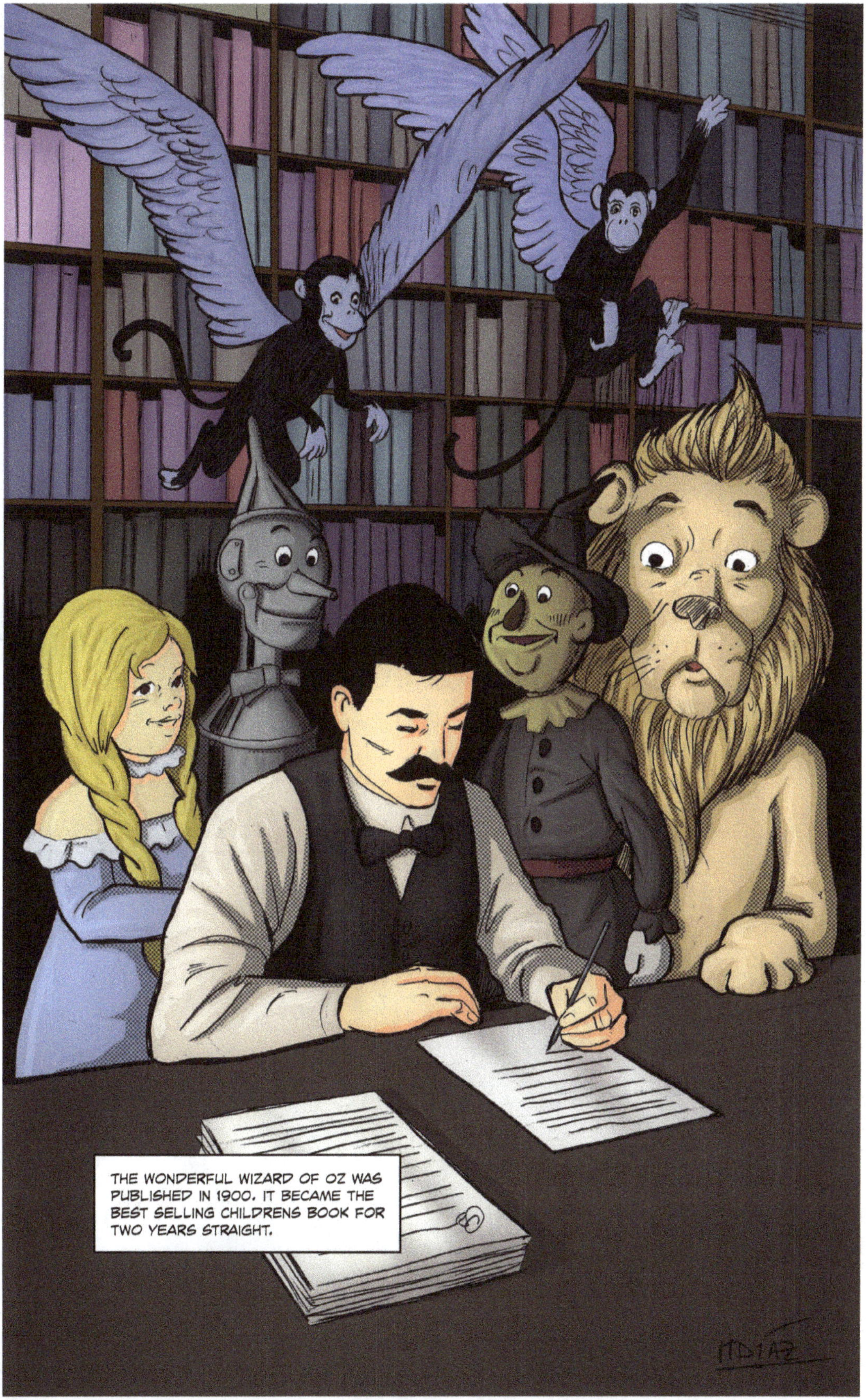
THE WONDERFUL WIZARD OF OZ WAS PUBLISHED IN 1900. IT BECAME THE BEST SELLING CHILDRENS BOOK FOR TWO YEARS STRAIGHT.

BAUM WAS UNSURE IF HIS CHILDRENS BOOK WOULD BE A SUCCESS BUT AT CHRISTMAS 1900 ALL HIS FEARS VANISHED. WHEN THEIR WASN'T ENOUGH MONEY FOR CHRISTMAS PRESENTS HE ASKED HIS PUBLISHER FOR AN ADVANCE ON HIS ROYALTIES.

A FAMILY STORY SAYS THAT MAUD BURNT THE SHIRT SHE WAS IRONING WHEN SHE OPENED THE CHECK.

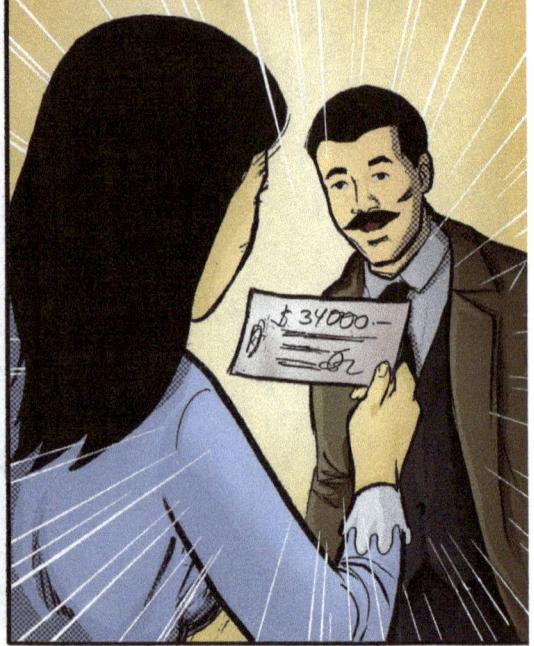

£ 34000·—

AFTER THE SUCCESS OF THE BOOK BAUM'S PUBLISHERS WERE CRYING OUT FOR A SEQUEL.

The WONDER-FUL WIZARD of OZ BY L. FRANK BAUM PICTURES BY W.W. DENSLOW

BUT BAUM DID NOT WANT TO MAKE A SEQUEL TO OZ. HE SET ABOUT CREATING OTHER CHILDRENS NOVELS SUCH AS DOT AND TOT OF MERRYLAND AND THE MASTERKEY WHICH FEATURED RAYGUNS AND TELEVISION SETS.

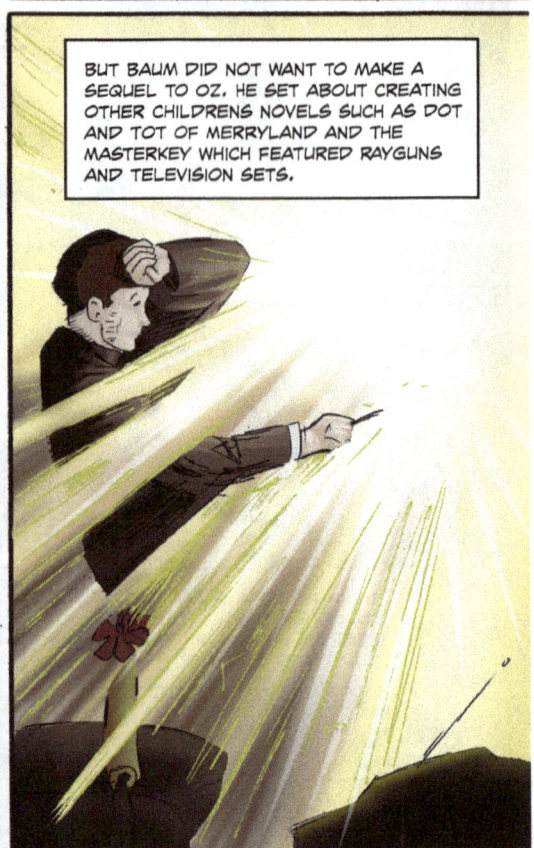

OF COURSE ONCE AGAIN THEATRE GOT A HOLD OF BAUM. HE TEAMED UP WITH COMPOSER PAUL TIETJENS AND DIRECTOR JULIAN MITCHELL TO CREATE A MUSICAL ABOUT OZ.

THE WIZARD OF OZ

RETITLED THE WIZARD OF OZ THE PLAY OPENED IN CHICAGO IN 1902 AND RAN UNTIL OCTOBER 1903.

BAUM WAS ASKED AGAIN TO WRITE A SEQUEL TO OZ. THIS TIME HE AGREED AND WROTE THE MARVELOUS LAND OF OZ WHICH TOLD THE ADVENTURES OF THE SCARECROW AND THE TINMAN.

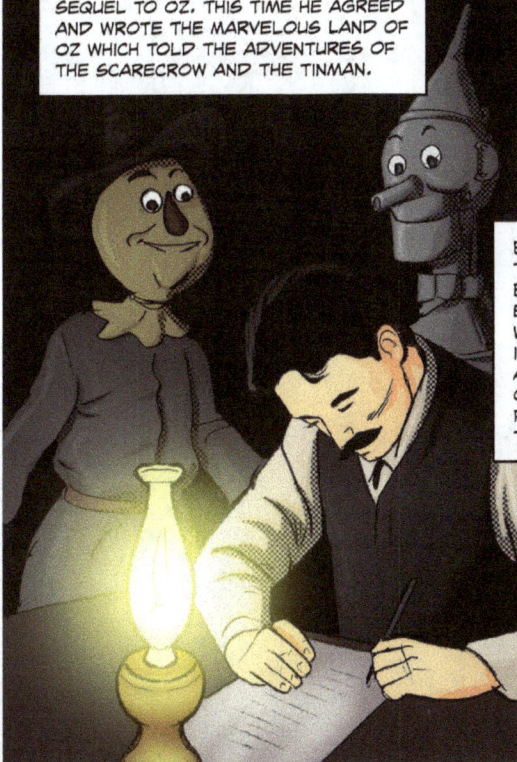

BAUM EVEN TRIED TO ADAPT THIS BOOK INTO A PLAY ENTITLED THE WOGGLE BUG BUT IT WAS TOO SOON AFTER THE WIZARD OF OZ AND THE PLAY WAS FORCED TO CLOSE.

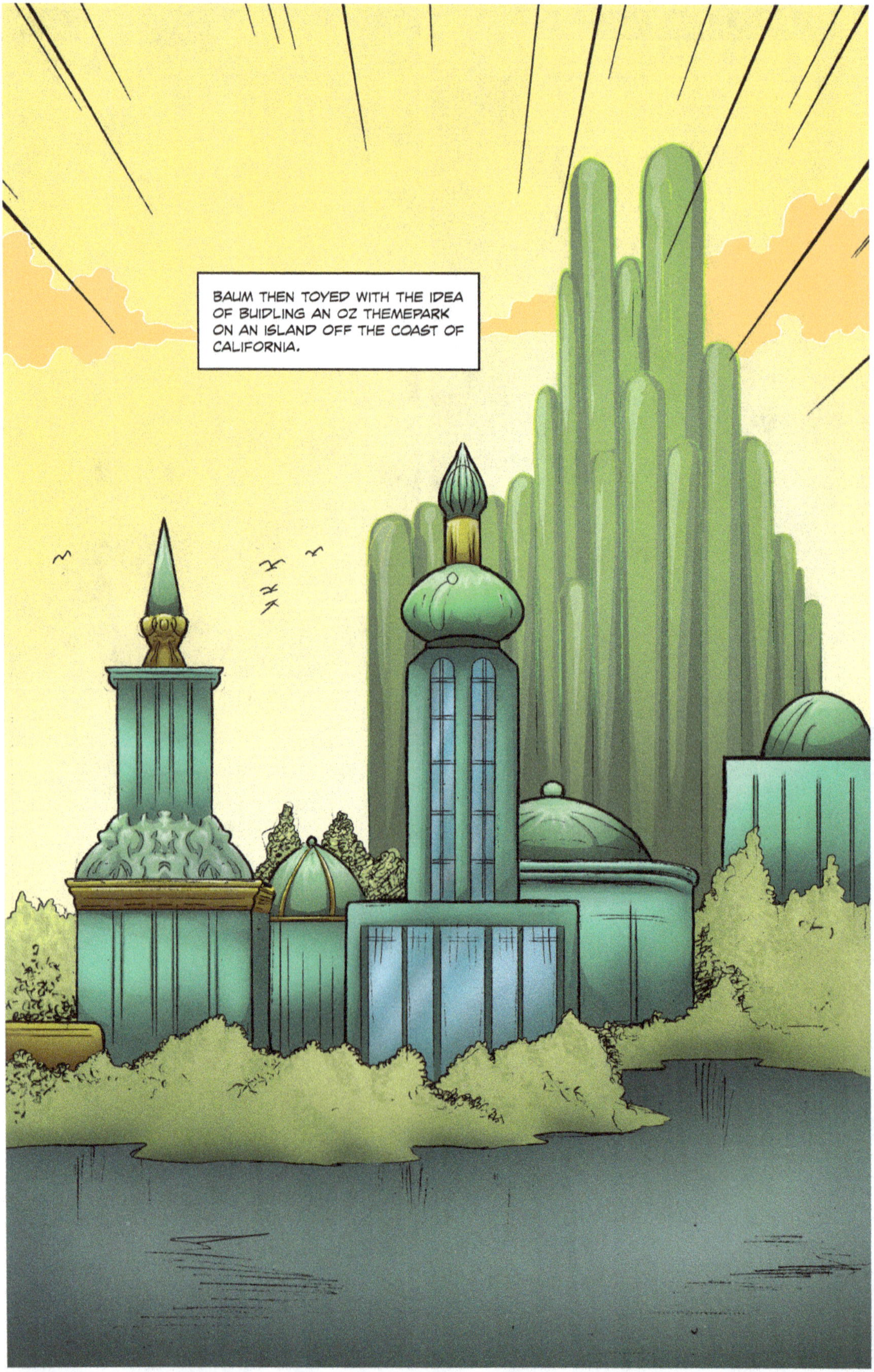
BAUM THEN TOYED WITH THE IDEA OF BUIDLING AN OZ THEMEPARK ON AN ISLAND OFF THE COAST OF CALIFORNIA.

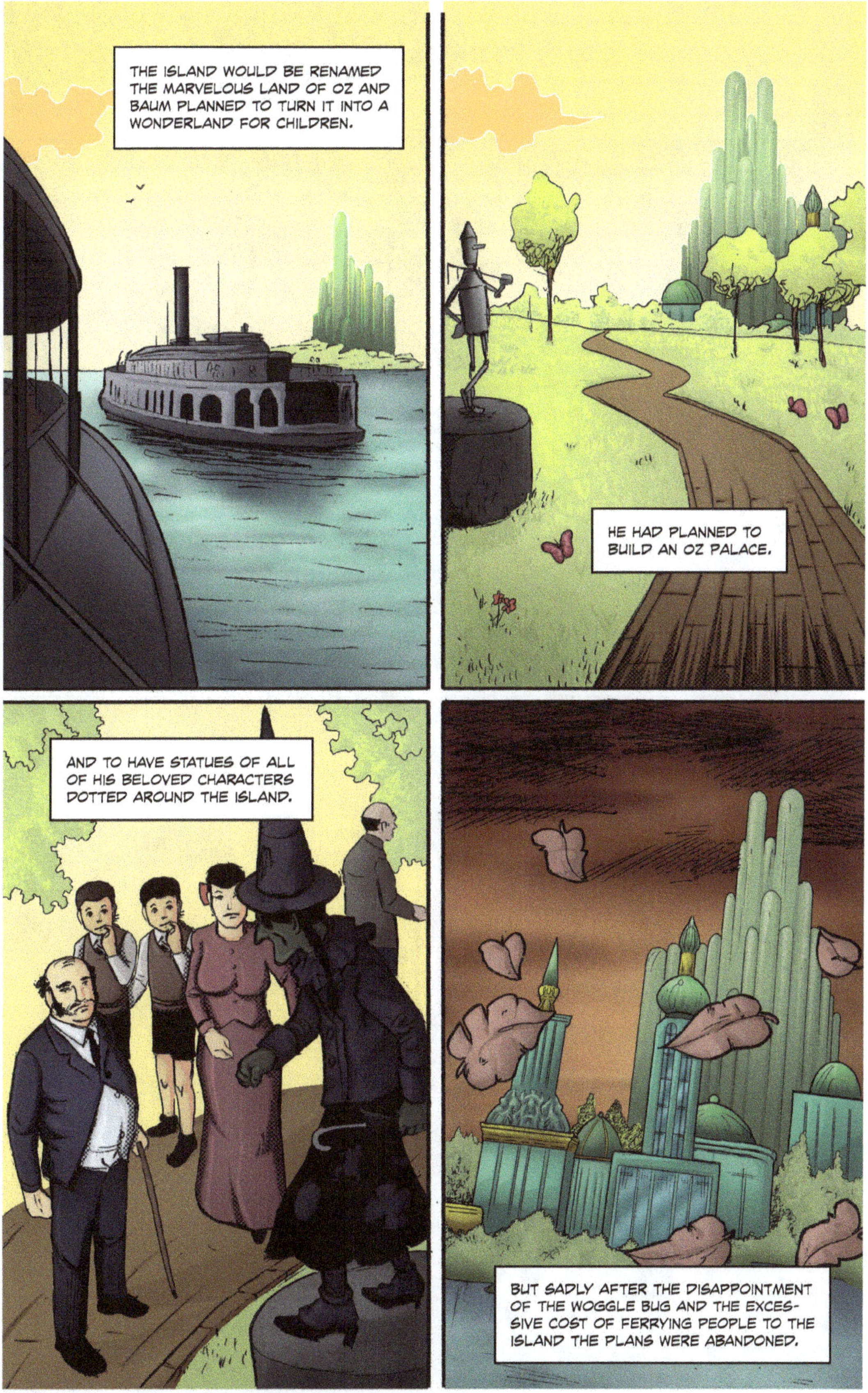
THE ISLAND WOULD BE RENAMED THE MARVELOUS LAND OF OZ AND BAUM PLANNED TO TURN IT INTO A WONDERLAND FOR CHILDREN.
HE HAD PLANNED TO BUILD AN OZ PALACE.
AND TO HAVE STATUES OF ALL OF HIS BELOVED CHARACTERS DOTTED AROUND THE ISLAND.
BUT SADLY AFTER THE DISAPPOINTMENT OF THE WOGGLE BUG AND THE EXCES-SIVE COST OF FERRYING PEOPLE TO THE ISLAND THE PLANS WERE ABANDONED.

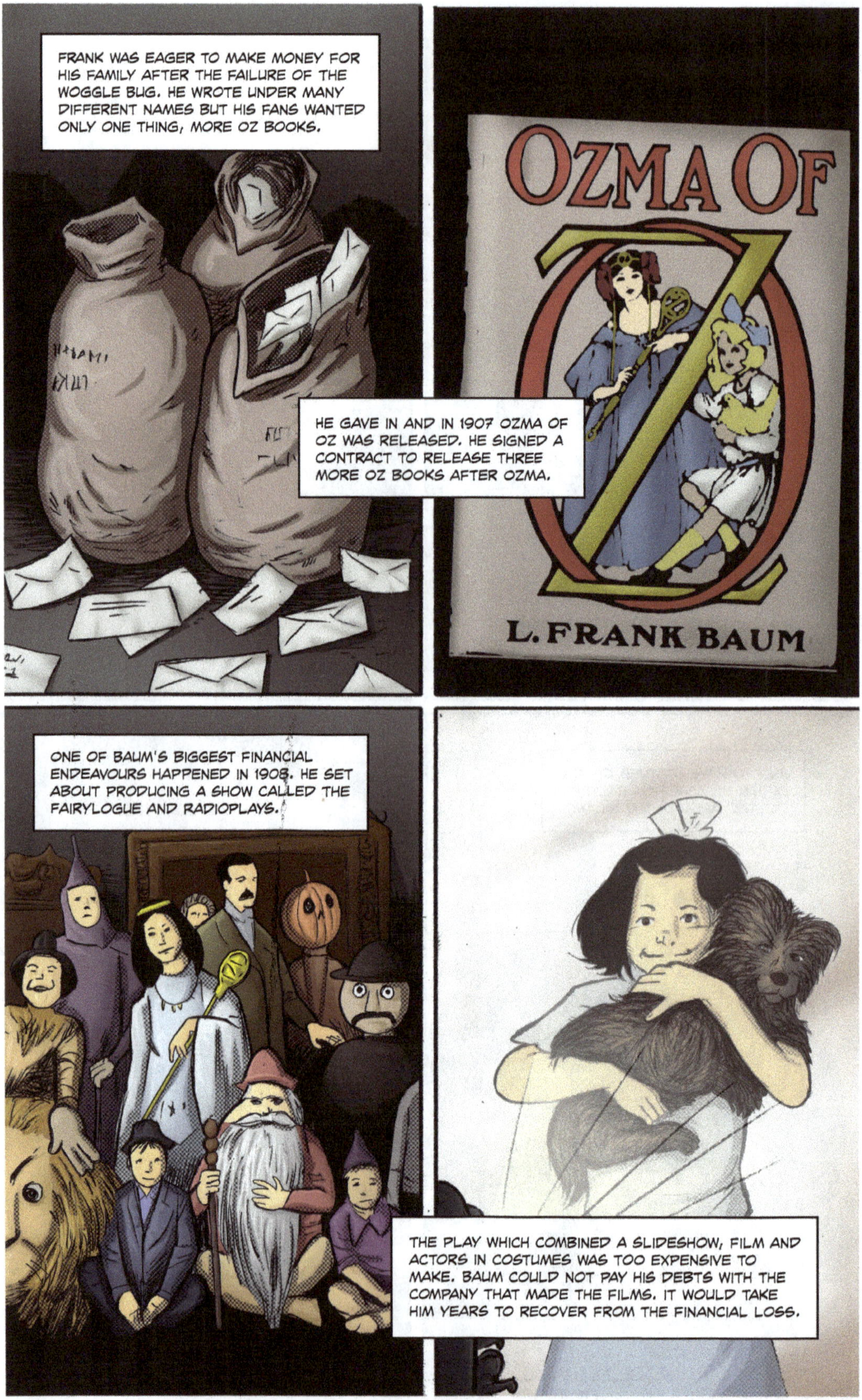
FRANK WAS EAGER TO MAKE MONEY FOR HIS FAMILY AFTER THE FAILURE OF THE WOGGLE BUG. HE WROTE UNDER MANY DIFFERENT NAMES BUT HIS FANS WANTED ONLY ONE THING, MORE OZ BOOKS.
OZMA OF OZ
L. FRANK BAUM
HE GAVE IN AND IN 1907 OZMA OF OZ WAS RELEASED. HE SIGNED A CONTRACT TO RELEASE THREE MORE OZ BOOKS AFTER OZMA.
ONE OF BAUM'S BIGGEST FINANCIAL ENDEAVOURS HAPPENED IN 1908. HE SET ABOUT PRODUCING A SHOW CALLED THE FAIRYLOGUE AND RADIOPLAYS.
THE PLAY WHICH COMBINED A SLIDESHOW, FILM AND ACTORS IN COSTUMES WAS TOO EXPENSIVE TO MAKE. BAUM COULD NOT PAY HIS DEBTS WITH THE COMPANY THAT MADE THE FILMS. IT WOULD TAKE HIM YEARS TO RECOVER FROM THE FINANCIAL LOSS.

MAUD STEPPED IN AND HELPED FRANK ONCE AGAIN. AFTER BAUM HAD TO SELL THE RIGHT OF MANY OF HIS BOOKS HE SHREWDLY TRANSFERRED MOST OF HIS PROPERTY INTO MAUD'S NAME. THIS MADE SURE THAT HE WOULD NOT LOOSE AS MUCH AS HE COULD HAVE.

BAUM RETURNED TO WORK IN THE THEATRE AND PRODUCED SEVERAL PLAYS FOR HARRY MARSTONS HALDERMAN'S SOCIAL CLUB THE UPLIFTERS.

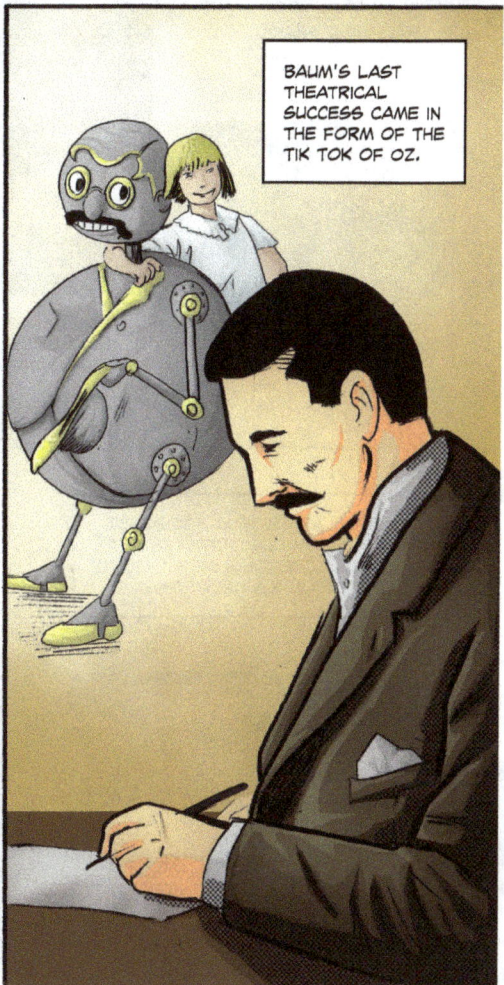

BAUM'S LAST THEATRICAL SUCCESS CAME IN THE FORM OF THE TIK TOK OF OZ.

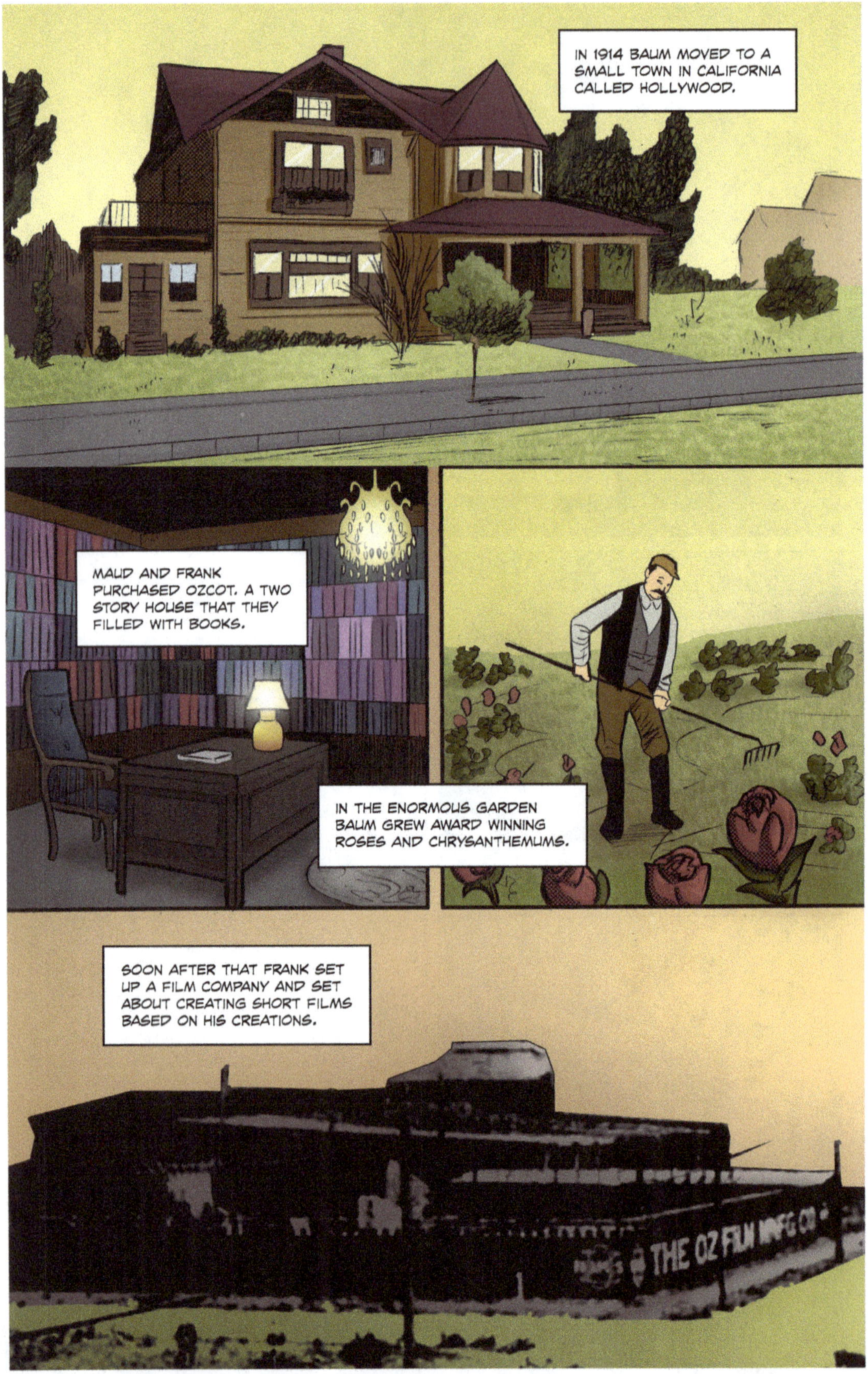
IN 1914 BAUM MOVED TO A SMALL TOWN IN CALIFORNIA CALLED HOLLYWOOD.
MAUD AND FRANK PURCHASED OZCOT. A TWO STORY HOUSE THAT THEY FILLED WITH BOOKS.
IN THE ENORMOUS GARDEN BAUM GREW AWARD WINNING ROSES AND CHRYSANTHEMUMS.
SOON AFTER THAT FRANK SET UP A FILM COMPANY AND SET ABOUT CREATING SHORT FILMS BASED ON HIS CREATIONS.
THE OZ FILM

THESE PRODUCTIONS WERE AHEAD OF THEIR TIME. THE DEMAND FOR CHILDRENS MOVIES HAD NOT BEEN REALISED AND SO THE COMPANY FOLDED.

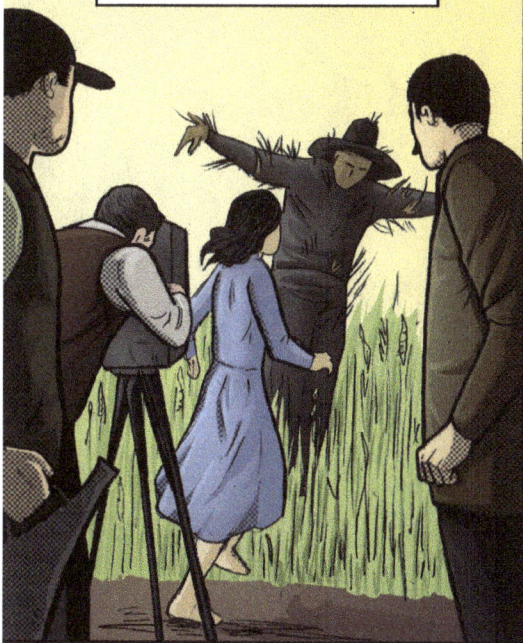

UNLIKE BEFORE BAUM DID NOT INVEST ANY OF HIS OWN MONEY INTO THE COMPANY BUT THE FAILURE OF THE COMPANY DID EFFECT BAUM'S FAILLING HEALTH.

BUT BAUM NEVER LOST HIS URGE TO ENTERTAIN. HE OPENED THE DOORS OF HIS HOME TO SCHOOL TOURS.

BAUM WOULD TELL CHILDREN STORIES FOR HOURS ON END.

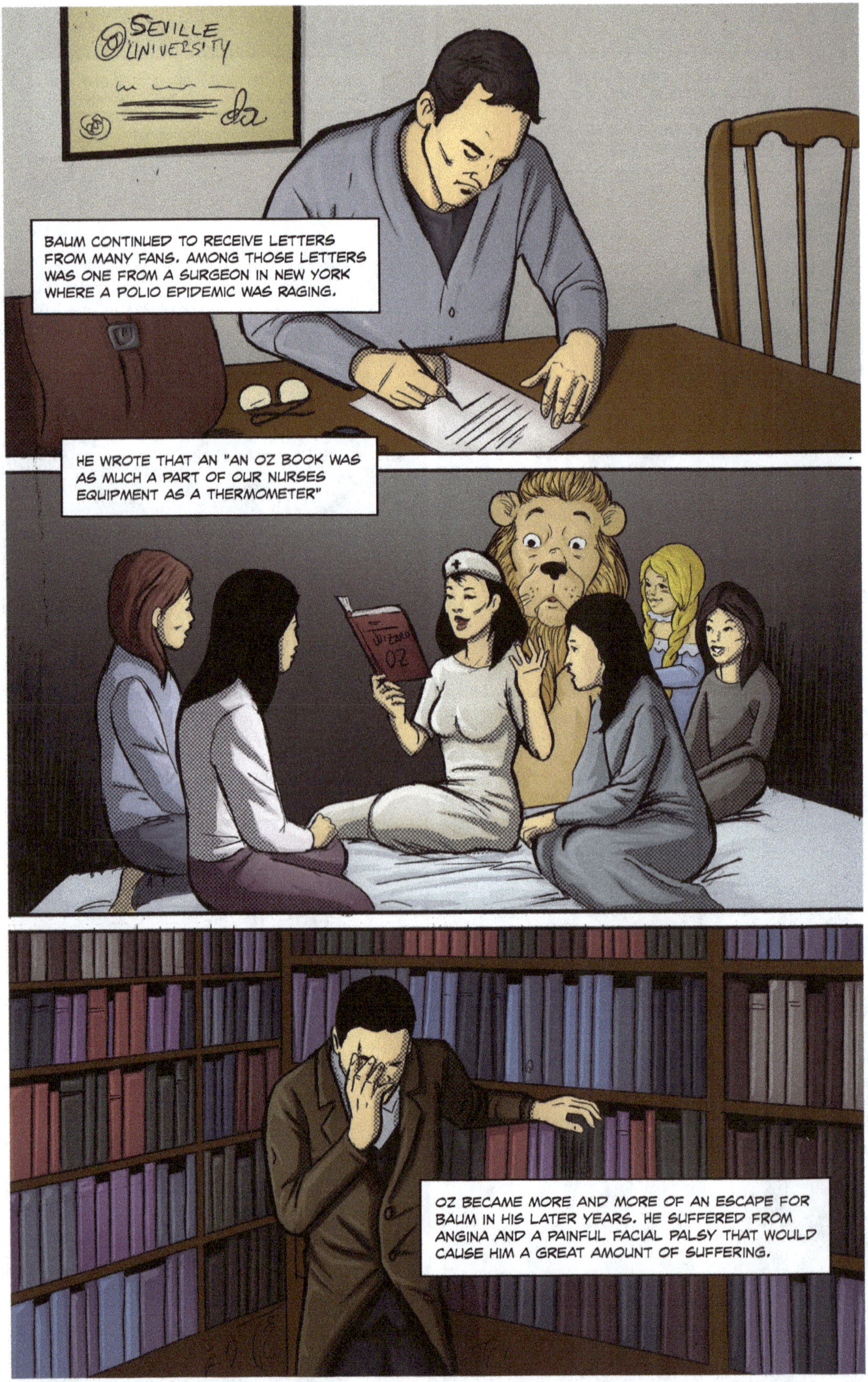
SEVILLE UNIVERSITY
BAUM CONTINUED TO RECEIVE LETTERS FROM MANY FANS. AMONG THOSE LETTERS WAS ONE FROM A SURGEON IN NEW YORK WHERE A POLIO EPIDEMIC WAS RAGING.
HE WROTE THAT AN "AN OZ BOOK WAS AS MUCH A PART OF OUR NURSES EQUIPMENT AS A THERMOMETER"
OZ BECAME MORE AND MORE OF AN ESCAPE FOR BAUM IN HIS LATER YEARS. HE SUFFERED FROM ANGINA AND A PAINFUL FACIAL PALSY THAT WOULD CAUSE HIM A GREAT AMOUNT OF SUFFERING.

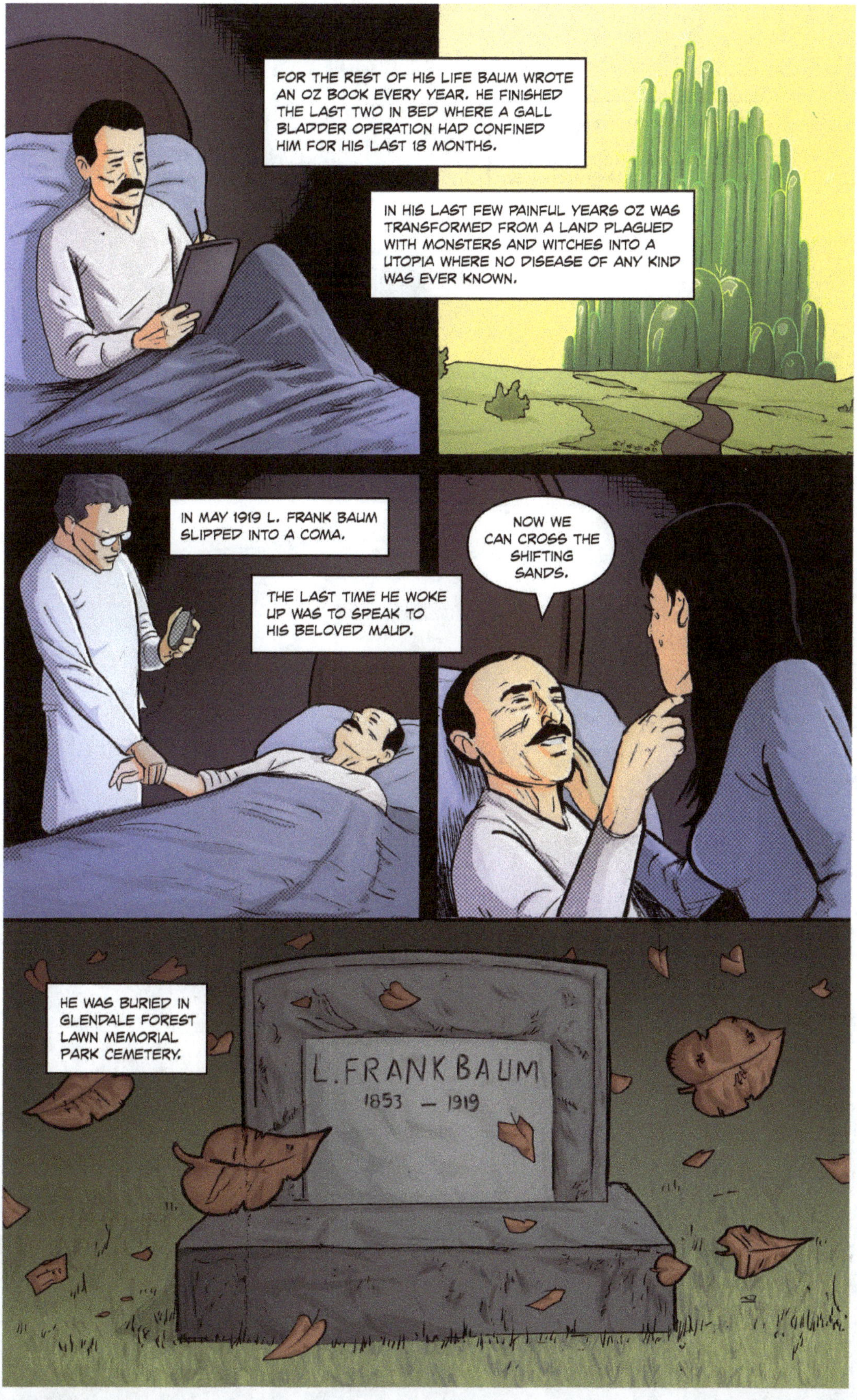
FOR THE REST OF HIS LIFE BAUM WROTE AN OZ BOOK EVERY YEAR. HE FINISHED THE LAST TWO IN BED WHERE A GALL BLADDER OPERATION HAD CONFINED HIM FOR HIS LAST 18 MONTHS.
IN HIS LAST FEW PAINFUL YEARS OZ WAS TRANSFORMED FROM A LAND PLAGUED WITH MONSTERS AND WITCHES INTO A UTOPIA WHERE NO DISEASE OF ANY KIND WAS EVER KNOWN.
IN MAY 1919 L. FRANK BAUM SLIPPED INTO A COMA.
THE LAST TIME HE WOKE UP WAS TO SPEAK TO HIS BELOVED MAUD.
NOW WE CAN CROSS THE SHIFTING SANDS.
HE WAS BURIED IN GLENDALE FOREST LAWN MEMORIAL PARK CEMETERY.
L. FRANK BAUM
1853 – 1919

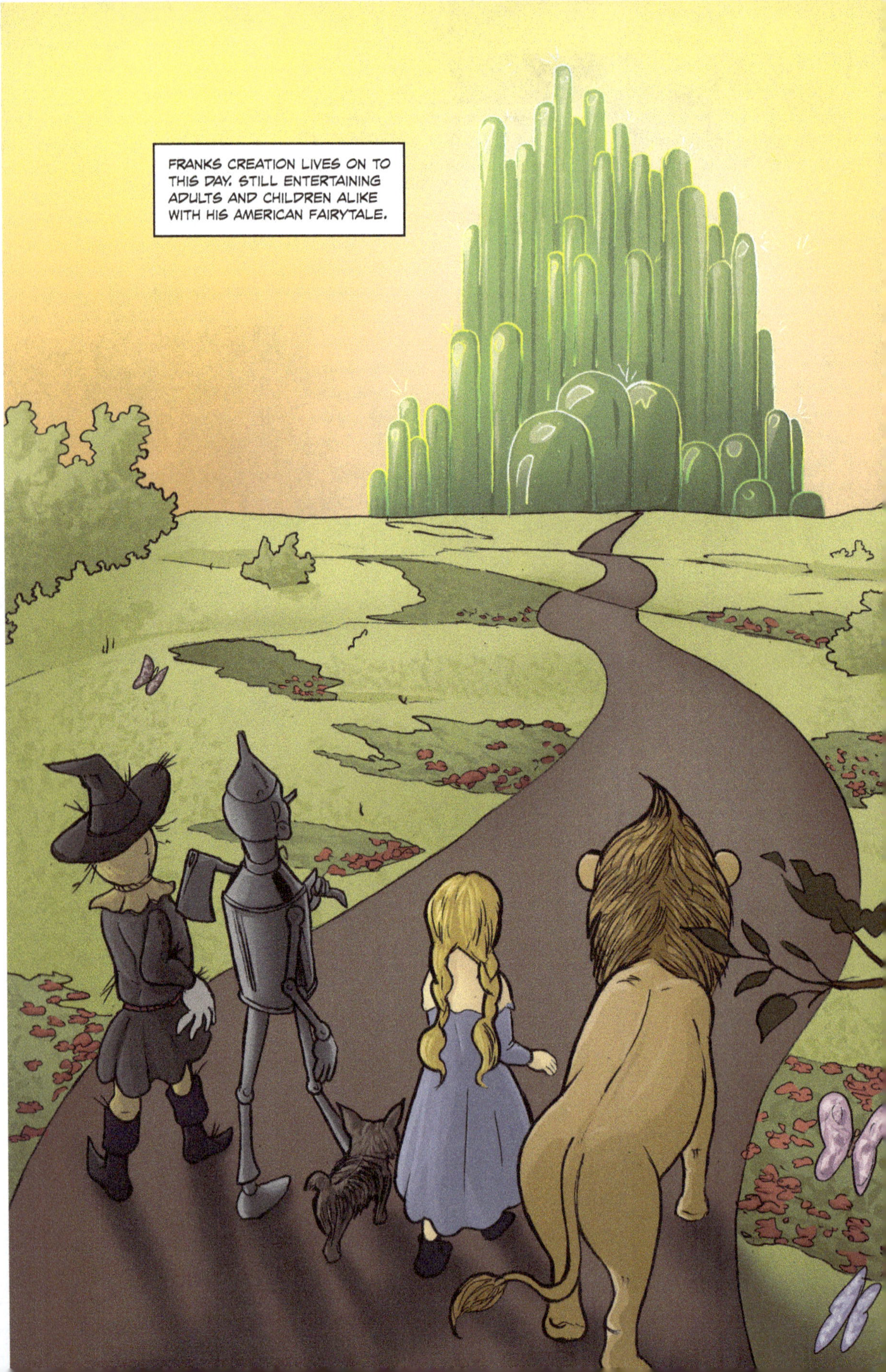
FRANKS CREATION LIVES ON TO THIS DAY. STILL ENTERTAINING ADULTS AND CHILDREN ALIKE WITH HIS AMERICAN FAIRYTALE.

BLUEWATER COMICS

Mike Lynch — **Writers**

Manuel Díaz — **Penciler**

Anvit Randeria — **Colorist**

David Hopkins — **Letterer**

Mario Gully — **Cover**

Darren G. Davis
Publisher

Jason Schultz
Vice President

Jarred Weisfeld
Literary Manager

Kailey Marsh
Entertainment Manager

Maggie Jessup
Publicity

Mary Higgins
Coordinator

Darren G. Davis
Production

BLUEWATER COMICS

www.bluewaterprod.com

PORTLAND'S

CONCERT

HALL

TOC
CONCERT HALL

www.ingramcontent.com/pod-product-compliance
Lightning Source LLC
Chambersburg PA
CBHW081236020426
42331CB00012B/3199